Sacred Solos

Level Four

Supplement to All Piano and Keyboard Methods

Compiled, Arranged and Edited by Wesley Schaum

Foreword

This series of sacred solos includes favorite hymns, gospel songs, spirituals and sacred music from the classical repertoire. The selections have been made to appeal to students of all ages and also with regard to popularity in many different churches. Some of the hymn tunes may be known with different titles and lyrics.

Contents

To access audio visit:
www.halleonard.com/mylibrary

1717-4954-9090-2676

ISBN 978-1-4950-8218-4

EXCLUSIVELY DISTRIBUTED BY
HAL•LEONARD®

Visit Hal Leonard Online at
www.halleonard.com

Contact us:
Hal Leonard
7777 West Bluemound Road
Milwaukee, WI 53213
Email: info@halleonard.com

In Europe, contact:
Hal Leonard Europe Limited
42 Wigmore Street
Marylebone, London, W1U 2RN
Email: info@halleonardeurope.com

In Australia, contact:
Hal Leonard Australia Pty. Ltd.
4 Lentara Court
Cheltenham, Victoria, 3192 Australia
Email: info@halleonard.com.au

How Great Thou Art

John W. Schaum

Swedish Folk Melody

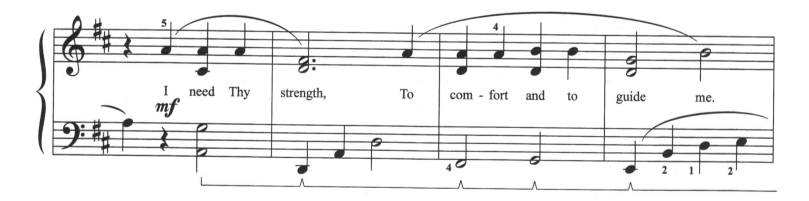

I sing to Thee   A   song of praise and   joy.

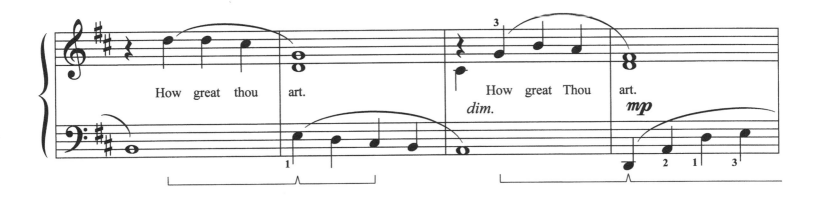

How great thou   art.   How great Thou   art.
dim.   *mp*

Thy peace and   love   Live   on   e - ter - nal - ly.
mf   *dim.*

How great Thou   art.   How great Thou   art.
mp cresc.   *f*   *rit.*   *mp*

When the Saints Go Marching In

American Folk Song

Con Brio ♩ = 96 - 104

Oh, when the Saints go march - ing in,

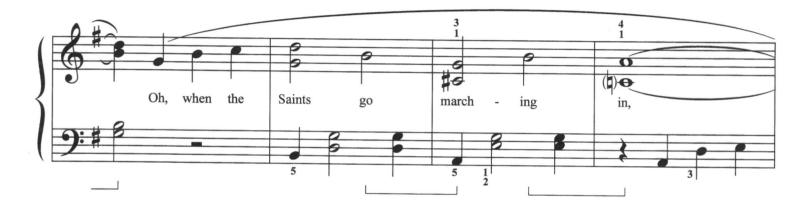

Oh, when the Saints go march - ing in,

Oh, Lord I want to be in that num - ber,

When the Saints go march - ing in.

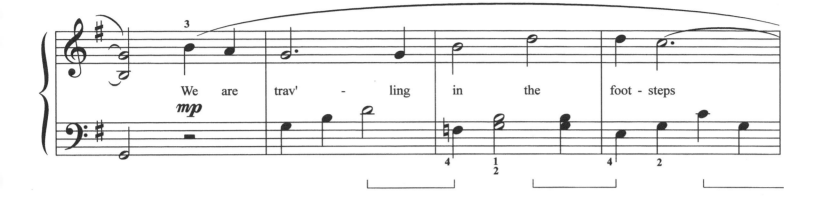

We are trav' - ling in the foot - steps

Of those who've gone be - fore,

And we'll all be re - u - nit - ed

On a new and sun - lit shore.

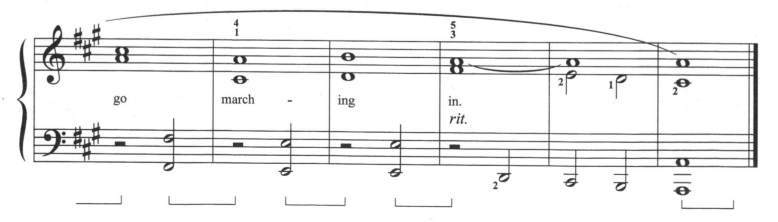

Rock of Ages

Augustus M. Toplady

Thomas Hastings

I Love To Tell the Story

Katherine Hankey

William G. Fischer

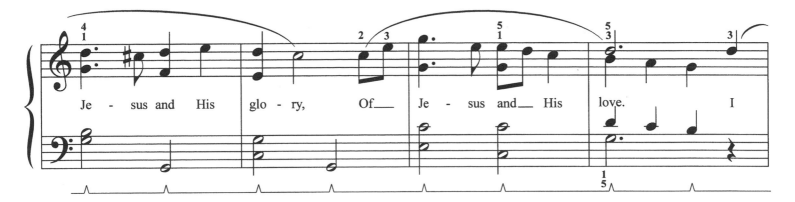

Je - sus and His glo - ry, Of___ Je - sus and___ His love. I

love to tell the sto - ry, Be - cause I know 'tis___ true; It

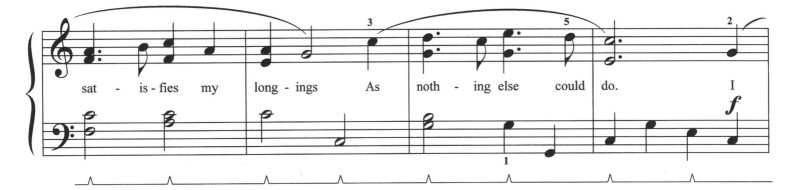

sat - is - fies my long - ings As noth - ing else could do. I

love to tell the sto - ry, 'Twill be my theme in glo - ry, To

tell the old,___ old sto - ry Of Je - sus and His love.

Softly and Tenderly

Will L. Thompson

Will L. Thompson

Dolce ♩ = 104 - 112

Soft - ly and ten - der - ly Je - sus is call - ing,

Call - ing for you and for me;

See, on the por - tals He's wait - ing and watch - ing,

Watch - ing for you and for me. Come

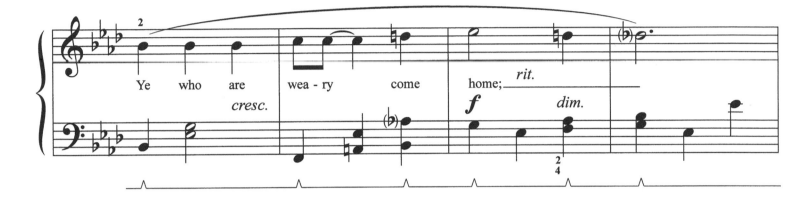

Song of Joy

John W. Schaum

Ludwig van Beethoven

Sing a song of joy and pray that peace will reign in ev - 'ry land,

Ev - 'ry race and ev - 'ry creed will meet and join with out - stretched hands.

Then to - geth - er work - ing and striv - ing hope - ful - ly seek - ing last - ing peace.

Joy - ful - ly each voice rings out in mu - sic that is great and grand.

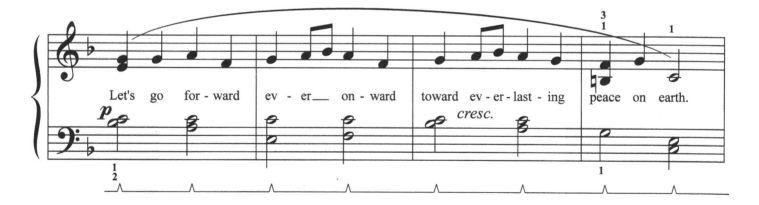

Crown Him With Many Crowns

Matthew Bridges

George J. Elvey

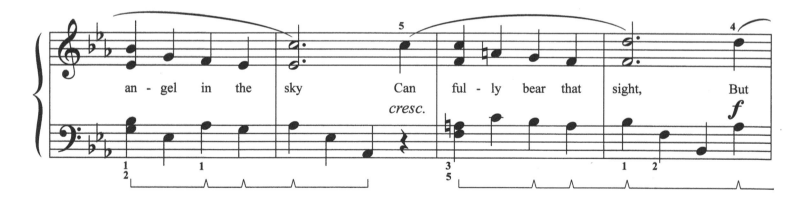

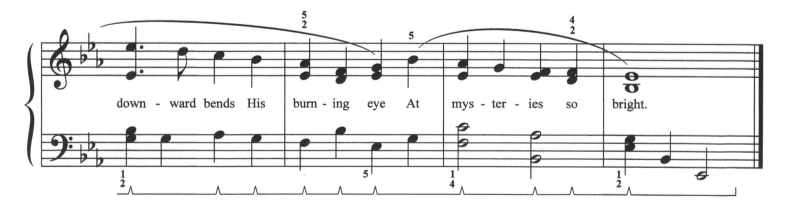

Sheep May Safely Graze

J.S. Bach

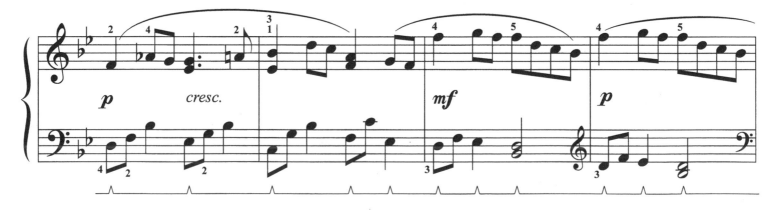

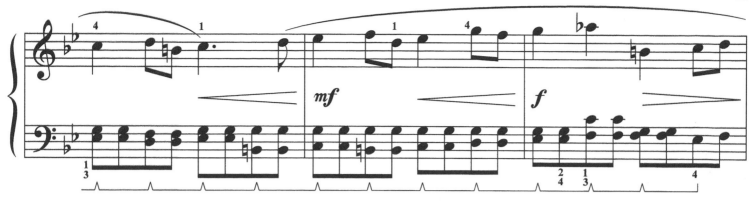

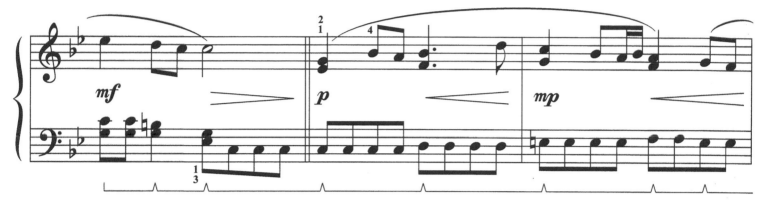

Onward Christian Soldiers

Sabine Baring-Gould

Arthur S. Sullivan

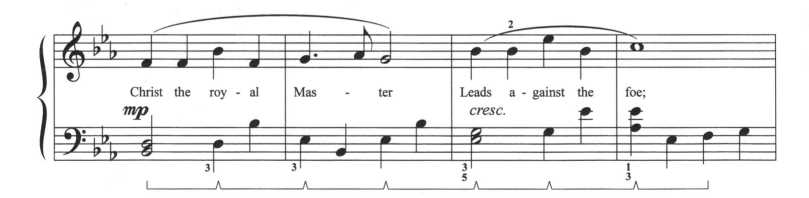

On - ward Chris - tian sol - diers,___ March - ing as to___ war,___

With the cross of Je - sus Go - ing on be - fore. *rit.*

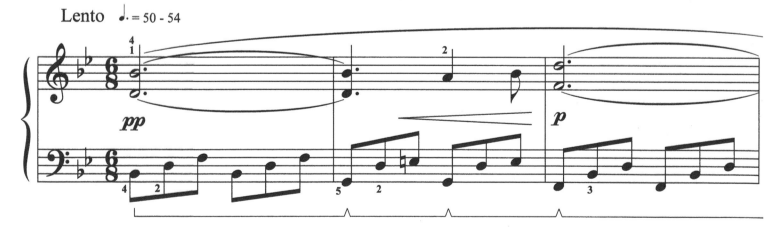

Ave Maria

Franz Schubert

Lento ♩. = 50 - 54

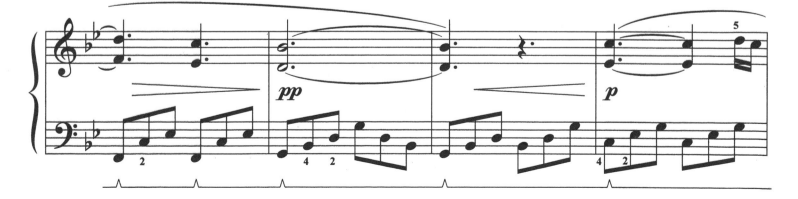

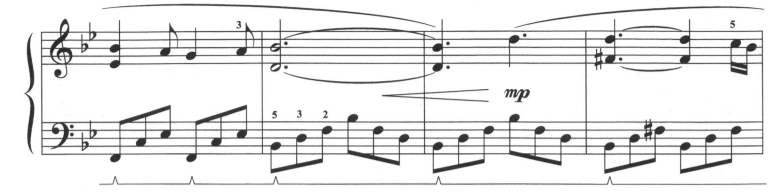

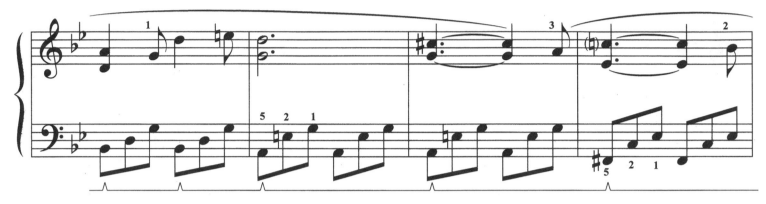

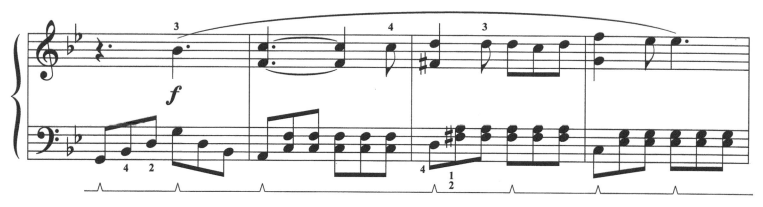
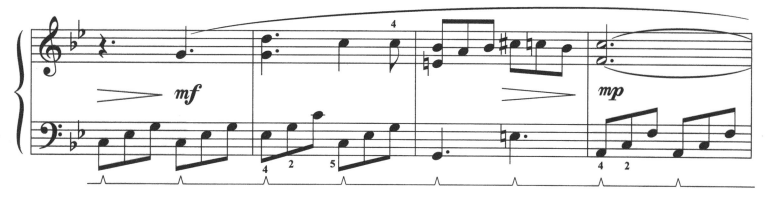
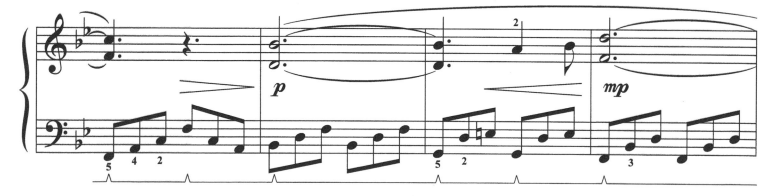
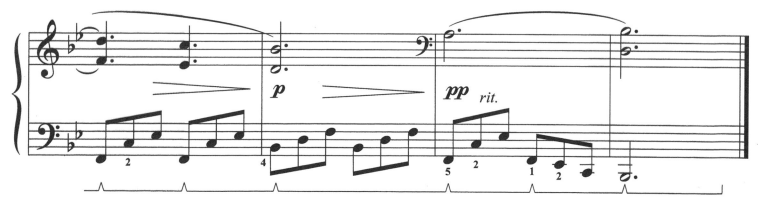

Hallelujah Chorus

George F. Handel

Andante ♩ = 76 - 84

MORE GREAT SCHAUM PUBLICATIONS

FINGERPOWER®

by John W. Schaum
Physical training and discipline are needed for both athletics and keyboard playing. Keyboard muscle conditioning is called technique. technique exercises are as important to the keyboard player as workouts and calisthenics are to the athlete. Schaum's *Fingerpower®* books are dedicated to development of individual finger strength and dexterity in both hands.

00645334	Primer Level – Book Only	$7.99
00645016	Primer Level – Book/Audio	$9.99
00645335	Level 1 – Book Only	$6.99
00645019	Level 1 – Book/Audio	$8.99
00645336	Level 2 – Book Only	$7.99
00645022	Level 2 – Book/Audio	$9.99
00645337	Level 3 – Book Only	$6.99
00645025	Level 3 – Book/Audio	$7.99
00645338	Level 4 – Book Only	$6.99
00645028	Level 4 – Book/Audio	$9.99
00645339	Level 5 Book Only	$7.99
00645340	Level 6 Book Only	$7.99

FINGERPOWER® ETUDES

Melodic exercises crafted by master technique composers. Modified or transposed etudes provide equal hand development with a planned variety of technical styles, keys, and time signatures.

00645392	Primer Level	$6.99
00645393	Level 1	$6.99
00645394	Level 2	$6.99
00645395	Level 3	$6.99
00645396	Level 4	$6.99

FINGERPOWER® FUN

arr. Wesley Schaum
Early Elementary Level
Musical experiences beyond the traditional *Fingerpower®* books that include fun-to-play pieces with finger exercises and duet accompaniments. Short technique preparatory drills (finger workouts) focus on melodic patterns found in each piece.

00645126	Primer Level	$6.95
00645127	Level 1	$6.99
00645128	Level 2	$6.95
00645129	Level 3	$6.99
00645144	Level 4	$6.95

FINGERPOWER® POP

arr. by James Poteat
10 great pop piano solo arrangements with fun technical warm-ups that complement the *Fingerpower®* series! Can also be used as motivating supplements to any method and in any learning situation.

00237508	Primer Level	$9.99
00237510	Level 1	$9.99
00282865	Level 2	$9.99
00282866	Level 3	$9.99
00282867	Level 4	$10.99

FINGERPOWER® TRANSPOSER

by Wesley Schaum
Early Elementary Level
This book includes 21 short, 8-measure exercises using 5-finger patterns. Positions are based on C,F, and G major and no key signatures are used. Patterns involve intervals of 3rds, 4ths, and 5ths up and down and are transposed from C to F and F to C, C to G and G to C, G to F and F to G.

00645150	Primer Level	$6.95
00645151	Level 1	$6.95
00645152	Level 2	$6.95
00645154	Level 3	$6.95
00645156	Level 4	$6.99

JUMBO STAFF MANUSCRIPT BOOK

This pad features 24 pages with 4 staves per page.

00645936		$4.25

CERTIFICATE OF MUSICAL ACHIEVEMENT

Reward your students for their hard work with these official 8x10-inch certificates that you can customize. 12 per package.

00645938		$6.99

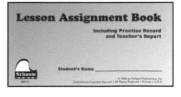

SCHAUM LESSON ASSIGNMENT BOOK

by John Schaum
With space for 32 weeks, this book will help keep students on the right track for their practice time.

00645935		$3.95

HAL•LEONARD®
www.halleonard.com